How many sheep can you count?

Which animal has just hatched?

Duck

Tractor

Hay

Barn

Can you spot the mouse?

How many monkeys can you count?

Tiger   Bear   Hippo   Crocodile

Can you spot the snake?

What's at the beach?

Can you spot three differences between the two sandcastles?

Towel   Sun   Shell   Seagull   Ice cream   Sandcastle

Can you find ten shells on the beach?

Which boat has a pink sail?

Hat

Dolphin

Bucket

Boat

Can you spot the crab?

What's in the garden?

How many apples
can you count?

Carrot   Cabbage   Snail   Bee   Butterfly   Watering can

Which bugs can fly?

Which type of vegetable is orange?

Can you spot the worm?

Tree

Flower

Bush

Bird

What's on the road?

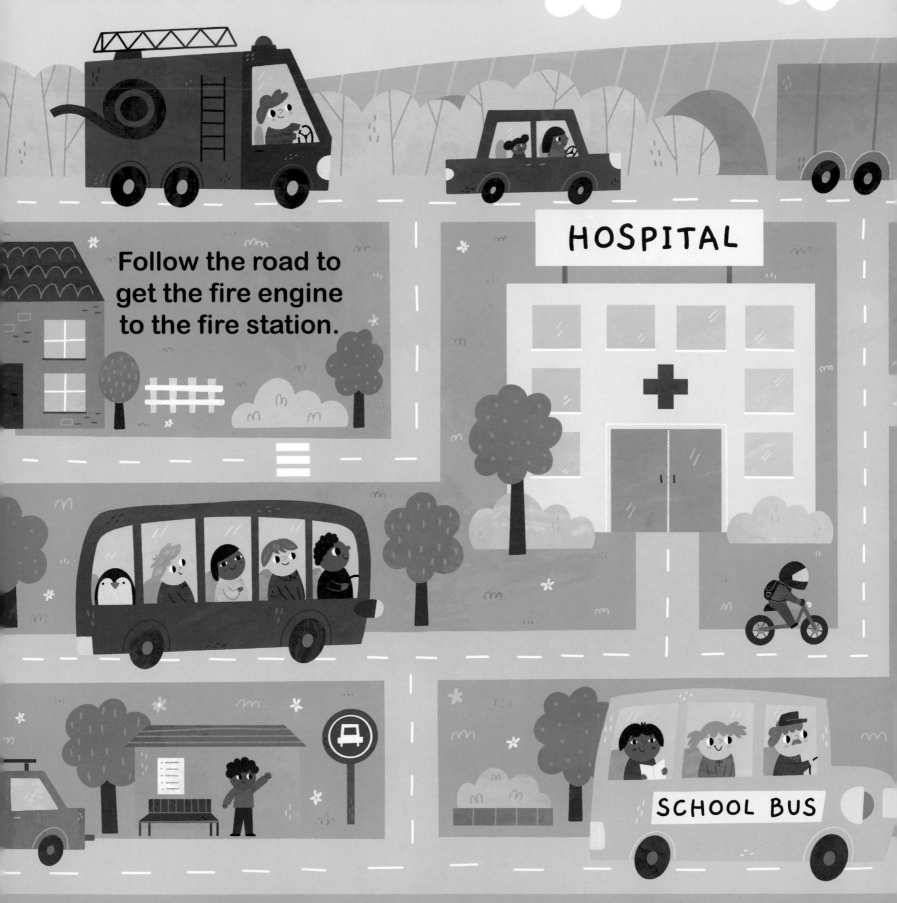

Follow the road to get the fire engine to the fire station.

HOSPITAL

SCHOOL BUS

Ambulance

Bus

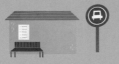
Bus stop

Car

Fire engine

Motorcycle

What's on the street?

What kind of weather do you like best?

How many windows can you count?

Bicycle  Puddle   Umbrella   Cloud  Coat   Lamppost

BAKERY

OPEN

What could you buy
from the bakery?

Plane   Boots   Rain   Window   Can you spot
the cat?

What's at the supermarket?

Where would you go to pay?

Apple

Bag

Basket

Cheese

Fish

Lettuce

How many potatoes can you count?

What type of food is an apple?

Can you spot the teddy bear?

 Meat

 Orange

 Potato

 Tomato

What's at the park?

What noise do dogs make?

Picnic Kite Swing Fountain Slide Dog

What would you take to a picnic?

Which person is flying the blue kite?

Can you spot the owl?

Roller skates

Swan

Bench

Ball

What's in the kitchen?

Which machine would you use to make toast?

How many cups are on the shelf?

Plate   Knife   Bowl   Fork   Bread   Spoon

What do you like to eat for breakfast?

Can you spot the hamster?

Toaster   Pan   Cup   Banana

What's in the bedroom?

What time of day is it?

What animal do the slippers look like?

| Lamp | Book | Bed | Clock | Slippers | Moon |

How many toys
are on the floor?

Can you spot
the doll?

Pencil　　Paints　　Stars　　Rug

What's at the party?

How many balloons can you count?

Gift

Party hat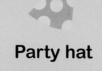

Balloon

Candle

Sandwich